JOHANNES BRAHMS

TRIO

for Piano, Violin and Horn
(or Violoncello or Viola)
E♭ major/Es-Dur/Mi♭ majeur
Op. 40

Ernst Eulenburg Ltd
London · Mainz · Madrid · New York · Paris · Prague · Tokyo · Toronto · Zürich

BRAHMS, PIANO TRIO, E FLAT, OP. 40

The Trio for Piano, Violin and Horn, an instrument which Brahms played in his youth and which he employs with such great effect in his Choruses for women's voices op. 17, was composed in the wooded neighbourhood of Lichtenthal, near Baden-Baden, in May 1865. Kalbeck, the learned and sound biographer of Brahms has disproved the theory that this essentially romantic Trio dates from the master's Detmold period, but Brahms probably rehearsed it first of all in Detmold in December 1865. The biographer has also rightly pointed out that the *Adagio mesto* (in E flat) is a lament over the death of the composer's mother and that the Chorale "Wer nur den lieben Gott läßt walten", somewhat akin to the folk-song "Dort in den Weiden steht ein Haus" is converted into the principal theme of the Finale.

The first performance took place in Karlsruhe on Dec. 7th 1865. Brahms played the piano part himself, as he also did on Jan. 10th 1866 at Oldenburg and at other places. He offered the work on June 18th 1866 to the publisher P. J. Simrock of Bonn, as a Trio for Pianoforte, Violin and Horn or Violoncello, remarking at the same time: — "The piece is to be played on the natural Horn and is not difficult for this instrument or either of the two others. My fee would be 16 Friedrichsdors." The publisher accepted the Trio which Brahms forwarded to him on July 4th. On Sep. 15th the composer returned the corrected proof and stipulated that the word "Waldhorn" (not Valve horn) should be printed on the title page. On Nov. 25th 1874 he remembered that no Piano arrangement for 4 hands had been made and offered to prepare one, but the publisher told him that the talented Robert Keller had already been commissioned to undertake the task.

On March 22nd 1884 Brahms wrote to Simrock as follows: — "My Horn-Trio should be provided with a Viola part instead of the 'Cello! With 'Cello it sounds dreadful*), but splendid with the Viola! The title should read: Horn or Viola!" The publisher was agreeable and Brahms wrote to him on Apr. 3rd: — "The Viola part must be issued separately. Herr Keller can easily see to that. I mean that the 'Cello part can be suppressed altogether." But this the publisher, quite rightly, was unwilling to do and continued to furnish the Trio with Horn, 'Cello and Viola parts.

We must not leave unmentioned what Clara Schumann wrote to Brahms about the performance of the work which she

---

*) This opinion however must be denied.

herself organized on Dec. 22nd 1866, namely:—"We had carefully studied your Trio and the Horn player was splendid! I don't think he cracked once, which is saying a good deal; it is true he used the valve horn; he could not be persuaded to play the "Waldhorn". The Scherzo was warmly applauded and the last movement very rousing, for it went like wild fire." The fact however that the magnificent work was a failure in Vienna when Clara Schumann played it there on Jan. 19th 1870, we gather from her Diary which says:—"They failed to understand the interesting and inspiring work, though the first movement for instance is full of suave melody, and the Finale full of life. The Adagio is also wonderful, but hard to understand at first hearing."

The Eulenburg edition of the miniature score which is now re-printed with these preliminary remarks has been obtainable since 1901.

Wilhelm Altmann

BRAHMS, KLAVIER-TRIO, ES DUR, OP. 40

Das Trio für Klavier, Violine und Waldhorn, ein Instrument, das Brahms in seiner Jugend geblasen und in seinen Gesängen für Frauenchor op. 17 sehr charakteristisch zur Begleitung (freilich in der Zweizahl) verwendet hatte, ist in den Wäldern von Lichtenthal bei Baden-Baden im Mai 1865 entstanden. Kalbeck, der so überaus gründliche Biograph des Meisters, hat die Legende zerstört, daß dieses echt romantische Trio bereits aus seiner Detmolder Zeit stammt, wohl aber hat es Brahms zuerst in Detmold im Dezember 1865 auf der Durchreise probiert. Sehr mit Recht hat Kalbeck auch darauf hingewiesen, daß das Adagio mesto (in *es*) eine Klage des Komponisten über den Tod seiner Mutter ist, daß darin schon das als Hauptthema des Finales verwertete niederrheinische, mit dem Choral „Wer nur den lieben Gott läßt walten" sich etwas berührende Volkslied „Dort in den Weiden steht ein Haus" angedeutet ist.

Die Uraufführung fand am 7. Dezember 1865 in Karlsruhe statt. Brahms spielte dabei das Klavier, ebenso am 10. Januar 1866 in Oldenburg und an anderen Orten. Erst am 18. Juni 1866 bot er dieses Werk dem Bonner Verlag P. J. Simrock an als Trio für Pianoforte, Violine und Horn oder Violoncell. Er bemerkte dazu: „Das Stück wurde (auch öffentlich) vom Hornisten auf dem einfachen Waldhorn geblasen, was denn wohl am deutlichsten sagt, daß es weder für das Instrument noch, da gerade dies sehr obligat ist, für die beiden anderen irgend schwierig ist. Das Honorar wäre 16 Friedrichsdors." Der Verlag nahm das Trio, das von Brahms ihm am 4. Juli übersandt wurde. Am 15. September schickte er bereits die Korrektur zurück und bemerkte nochmals, daß Waldhorn (nicht Horn = Ventilhorn) auf dem Titel stehen sollte. Am 25. November 1874 erinnerte er sich daran, daß von diesem Werke noch keine Bearbeitung für Klavier zu 4 Händen erschienen war, und erbot sich zu dieser, doch erfuhr er dann von dem Verleger, daß dieser damit bereits den bewährten Robert Keller beauftragt hatte.

Am 22. März 1884 schrieb er an den Verleger: „Mein Horn-Trio sollte eigentlich eine Bratschenstimme statt der Violoncellstimme mitkriegen! Mit Cello nämlich klingt es abscheulich*), mit Bratsche ausgezeichnet! Das könnte ausdrücklich auf dem Titel stehen: Horn oder Bratsche!" Der Verleger war selbstverständlich dazu bereit. Brahms schrieb ihm darauf am 3. April: „Die Bratschenstimme für das Horn-Trio müßte extra geschrieben, resp. gestochen werden.

*) Dieser Ansicht von Brahms muß aber durchaus widersprochen werden.

Herr Keller kann das leicht besorgen. Ich meine, dic Violoncellstimme könnte dann ganz wegfallen." Sehr mit Recht aber verstand sich der Verleger hierzu nicht, sondern gab das Trio von nun an gleichzeitig mit einer Horn-, Violoncell- und Bratschenstimme in den Handel.

Nicht unerwähnt sei, was Klara Schumann über die von ihr veranstaltete Leipziger Aufführung dieses Trios am 22. Dezember 1866 an Brahms geschrieben hat, nämlich: „Dein Trio ... hatten wir schön einstudiert, und der Hornist war vortrefflich! Ich glaube, er hat nicht einmal gekickst, und das will doch viel sagen; freilich hatte er Ventilhorn, zum Waldhorn war er nicht zu bringen. Das Scherzo wurde am lebhaftesten applaudiert, dann aber zündete der letzte Satz, der wie aus der Pistole geschossen ging." Daß aber das herrliche Werk, als Klara Schumann es am 19. Januar 1870 in Wien spielte, gar nicht gefiel, lesen wir in ihrem Tagebuch, wo sie noch hinzufügt: „Sie verstanden das wahrhaft geistvolle, durch und durch interessante Werk nicht, trotzdem der erste Satz z. B. voll der einschmeichelndsten Melodien ist und der letzte Satz wieder voll frischen Lebens. Das Adagio ist wundervoll auch, allerdings für das Erstemalhören schwer."

Die kleine Partitur des Verlags Eulenburg, die jetzt mit diesen einleitenden Bemerkungen neu gedruckt worden ist, ist seit 1901 im Handel.

Wilhelm Altmann

TRIO

I.

Johannes Brahms, Op. 40.
1833-1897

No. 249 E. E. 4583 Ernst Eulenburg Ltd

cresc.
cresc.
cresc.

40

50
f
dim.
f
dim.
dim.

p
p
p

60
poco cresc.
poco cresc.
poco cresc.

70
dim.
dim.
dim.

Poco più animato.
mp
Poco più animato.
senza rit.
mp

80
p

90

f
f legato

cresc.
cresc.
p

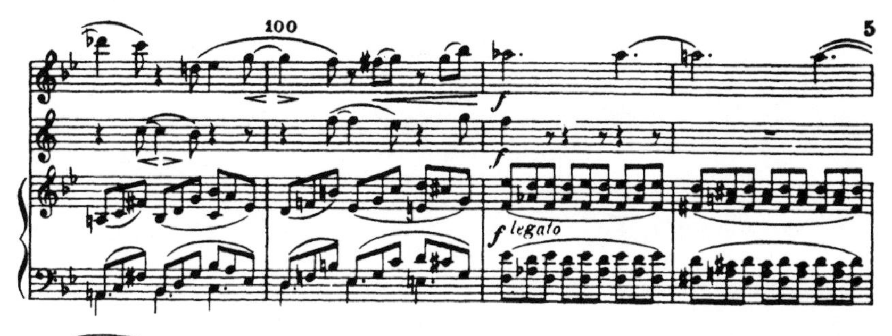
100
f
f
f legato

f
fp
f
fp
f
p dolce

110
dolce
legato

sempre cresc.
sempre cresc.
sempre cresc.

p
p
sf
sf
p
sf

120
p
p
sf
sf
p
sf

p
dim.
poco a poco rit.
p
dim.
poco a poco rit.
p
dim.
poco a poco rit.

130
Ped.
Ped.

Tempo I.
Tempo I.
p dolce

140
dolce

p

150
poco cresc.
poco cresc.
poco cresc.

dim.
160
dim.
dim.

mezzo p espress.
3
3
senza rit.

Poco più animato.
170
p
Poco più animato.
mezzo p

180
sempre cresc.
sempre cresc.
sempre cresc.

p

190
sf
p
sf
p

sf
p
dim.
poco a poco rit.
sf
p
dim.
poco a poco rit.

p
pp

200 Tempo I.
Tempo I.
pp

210
poco cresc.
poco cresc.

220
espress. sempre cresc.
un poco a-
ad lib.
un poco a-
p
sempre cresc.
nimato poi a poi
nimato poi a poi
f
230
f espress.
ad lib.
f legato

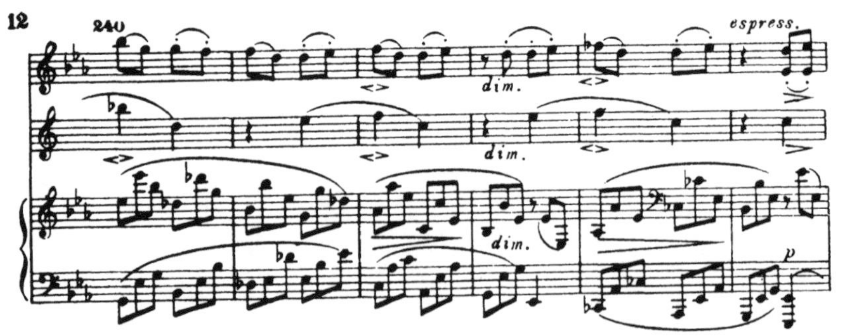
240
espress.
dim.
dim.
dim.
p

250
sempre dim. e ritar - dando poco a

poco

260
8
pp

II. Scherzo.

cresc.
mf cresc.
cresc.

80
p

90
p

100
cresc.
f
p

110
p
f

120
p dolce
p dolce
leggiero
p

130

140
p
p

150

cresc.
cresc.

160
f
f

170
f
f
f
f

180

190
fp
p
p

200
p
p

210
p

220
poco a poco cresc.
poco a poco cresc.

230
f
f
f
fz
fz

240
f
f
mf

250
sf
sf
f
sf
sf

p

260
cresc.
cresc.

270
Fine.
Fine.

280
p
rit. poco a poco
p
p rit. poco a poco

Molto meno Allegro.
290
p espress.
p espress.
Molto meno Allegro.
p
300
310
p
p

poco a poco cresc.

320

p espress.
p

330
cresc.
cresc.
Ped.

Scherzo da capo sin' al Fine.

Adagio mesto.
III.
p espress.
p espress.
Adagio mesto.
p una corda
p
t. c.
10
una c.
p
espress.
pp
p una corda
20
sempre p
p
sempre p e legato

p sempre e legato
30
dim.
pp
cresc.
un poco stringendo
p
sfp

poco
40
a
dim.
poco
in tempo
ppp quasi niente
pp una corda
p espress.
p
50

60
molto p
p
pp
pp
pp
pp
poco accell.
f passionata
poco accell.
f passionata
cre - scen - do
poco accell.
f

70

ff
ff
ff

poco rit.
tempo primo
poco rit.
tempo primo
poco rit.
tempo primo
dim.

80
pp
sf
sf
sf
p
p
p

IV. Finale.

Allegro con brio.
p
cresc.
Allegro con brio.
p
stacc.
10
mf
f
mf
cresc.
cresc.
f
f
f
20

30
f
f
non legato

40
f
f

fp
fp
p
p

50

marcato

60

70

pp
dim.
dim.
80
pp
pp
p dolce
pp
p dol.
90
1.
p
cresc.
mf cresc.
mf
cresc.
f
f

2.
f
p cresc.
f

100
f non legato
fz
fp

p espr.
p espr.

110
p
p

120

poco a poco cresc.
poco a poco cresc.
poco a poco cresc.

130

140
rit. poco a
p
rit. poco a
f
rit. poco a
p
poco
poco
poco
dim.
150
poco a poco
cresc. poco a poco
p accel. e cresc. poco a poco
160
p in tempo
in tempo
f
p in tempo

cresc.
f
mf

170
cresc.
cresc.

180
f
f
f

190
non legato
200
210

marcato
f

220
f

230
p dolce
p
fp

più p
più p
p dolce

240
dim.
pp
pp
p dolce
p
dolce p
250
cresc.
p cresc.
cresc.
f
f
260
f
f
f

270

280